SAVANNAH
RESTAURANT GUIDE

RESTAURANTS, BARS AND CAFES
Your Guide to Authentic Regional Eats

GUIDE BOOK FOR TOURIST

SAVANNAH RESTAURANT GUIDE 2022
Best Rated Restaurants in Savannah, Georgia

© Croswell B. Brown
© E.G.P. Editorial

Printed in USA.

ISBN-13: 9798503356700

SAVANNAH RESTAURANT GUIDE

The Most Recommended Restaurants in Savannah

This directory is dedicated to the Business Owners and Managers who provide the experience that the locals and tourists enjoy. Thanks you very much for all that you do and thank for being the "People Choice".

Thanks to everyone that posts their reviews online and the amazing reviews sites that make our life easier.

The places listed in this book are the most positively reviewed and recommended by locals and travelers from around the world.

Thank you for your time and enjoy the directory that is designed with locals and tourist in mind!

TOP 500
RESTAURANTS
Ranked from #1 to #500

#1
Sweet Spice
Cuisines: Caribbean
Average price: Inexpensive
Address: 5515 Waters Ave
Savannah, GA 31404
Phone: (912) 335-8146

#2
Savannah Seafood Shack
Cuisines: Seafood
Average price: Modest
Address: 116 E Broughton St
Savannah, GA 31401
Phone: (912) 344-4393

#3
Cotton & Rye
Cuisines: American
Average price: Modest
Address: 1801 Habersham St
Savannah, GA 31401
Phone: (912) 777-6286

#4
Hitch
Cuisines: American
Average price: Modest
Address: 300 Drayton St
Savannah, GA 31401
Phone: (912) 239-6970

#5
Sandfly BBQ At The Streamliner
Cuisines: Barbeque
Average price: Modest
Address: 1220 Barnard St
Savannah, GA 31401
Phone: (912) 335-8058

#6
Maté Factor
Cuisines: Bakery, Sandwiches
Average price: Inexpensive
Address: 401 E Hall St
Savannah, GA 31401
Phone: (912) 235-2906

#7
Sly's Sliders and Fries
Cuisines: Burgers, Hot Dogs
Average price: Inexpensive
Address: 1710 Abercorn St
Savannah, GA 31401
Phone: (912) 239-4219

#8
Zunzi's Takeout & Catering
Cuisines: Vegetarian, South African
Average price: Inexpensive
Address: 108 E York St
Savannah, GA 31401
Phone: (912) 443-9555

#9
Elizabeth On 37th
Cuisines: American
Average price: Expensive
Address: 105 E 37th St
Savannah, GA 31401
Phone: (912) 236-5547

#10
Joe's Homemade Cafe
Cuisines: Deli, Bakery, Cafe
Average price: Inexpensive
Address: 5515 Waters Ave
Savannah, GA 31404
Phone: (912) 349-0251

#11
Narobia's Grits & Gravy
Cuisines: Soul Food, Southern
Average price: Inexpensive
Address: 2019 Habersham St
Savannah, GA 31401
Phone: (912) 231-0563

#12
The Olde Pink House Restaurant
Cuisines: Southern
Average price: Expensive
Address: 23 Abercorn St
Savannah, GA 31401
Phone: (912) 232-4286

#13
Green Truck Neighborhood Pub
Cuisines: Pub, Burgers, American
Average price: Modest
Address: 2430 Habersham St
Savannah, GA 31401
Phone: (912) 234-5885

#14
Treylor Park
Cuisines: American, Bar
Average price: Modest
Address: 115 E Bay St
Savannah, GA 31401
Phone: (912) 495-5557

#15
Alligator Soul
Cuisines: Southern, Cajun/Creole, American
Average price: Expensive
Address: 114 Barnard St
Savannah, GA 31401
Phone: (912) 232-7899

#16
The Public Kitchen & Bar
Cuisines: American, Bar, Burgers
Average price: Modest
Address: 1 W Liberty St
Savannah, GA 31401
Phone: (912) 200-4045

#17
Crystal Beer Parlor
Cuisines: Southern, American, Burgers
Average price: Modest
Address: 301 W Jones St
Savannah, GA 31401
Phone: (912) 349-1000

#18
The Ordinary Pub
Cuisines: American, Gastropub
Average price: Modest
Address: 217 1/2 W Broughton St
Savannah, GA 31401
Phone: (912) 238-5130

#19
Starland Cafe
Cuisines: Sandwiches, Cafe
Average price: Modest
Address: 11 E 41st St
Savannah, GA 31401
Phone: (912) 443-9355

#20
The Collins Quarter
Cuisines: Cafe, American
Average price: Modest
Address: 151 Bull St
Savannah, GA 31401
Phone: (912) 777-4147

#21
Sweet Potatoes Kitchen
Cuisines: Southern, Soul Food, Caribbean
Average price: Modest
Address: 6825 Waters Ave
Savannah, GA 31406
Phone: (912) 352-3434

#22
Savannah's Fresh Catch Seafood
Cuisines: Seafood, Seafood Market
Average price: Inexpensive
Address: 1201 Habersham St
Savannah, GA 31401
Phone: (912) 233-3696

#23
The Vault Kitchen and Market
Cuisines: Sushi Bar, Bar, Asian Fusion
Average price: Modest
Address: 2112 Bull St
Savannah, GA 31401
Phone: (912) 201-1950

#24
Planters Tavern
Cuisines: Bar, Southern, Diner
Average price: Expensive
Address: 23 Abercorn St
Savannah, GA 31412
Phone: (912) 232-4286

#25
Local 11 Ten
Cuisines: American
Average price: Expensive
Address: 1110 Bull St
Savannah, GA 31401
Phone: (912) 790-9000

#26
22 Square Restaurant & Bar
Cuisines: American
Average price: Modest
Address: 14 Barnard St
Savannah, GA 31401
Phone: (912) 629-9493

#27
B Matthew's Eatery
Cuisines: American, Breakfast & Brunch
Average price: Modest
Address: 325 E Bay St
Savannah, GA 31401
Phone: (912) 233-1319

#28
Back in the Day Bakery
Cuisines: Bakery, Coffee & Tea, Sandwiches
Average price: Modest
Address: 2403 Bull St
Savannah, GA 31401
Phone: (912) 495-9292

#29
Betty Bombers
Cuisines: American, Burgers, Cheesesteaks
Average price: Modest
Address: 1108 Bull St
Savannah, GA 31401
Phone: (912) 272-9326

#30
Foxy Loxy Cafe
Cuisines: Coffee & Tea, Desserts, Cafe
Average price: Inexpensive
Address: 1919 Bull St
Savannah, GA 31401
Phone: (912) 401-0543

#31
The Grey
Cuisines: American
Average price: Expensive
Address: 109 Martin Luther King Jr Blvd
Savannah, GA 31401
Phone: (912) 662-5999

#33
In Vino Veritas
Cuisines: Wine Bar, Tapas/Small Plates
Average price: Modest
Address: 102 E Liberty St
Savannah, GA 31401
Phone: (912) 662-6665

#32
The Flying Monk Noodle Bar
Cuisines: Vietnamese, Noodles
Average price: Modest
Address: 5 W Broughton St
Savannah, GA 31401
Phone: (912) 232-8888

#34
Persepolis Lounge and Grill
Cuisines: Persian/Iranian, Greek, Hookah Bar
Average price: Modest
Address: 41 Whitaker St
Savannah, GA 31401
Phone: (912) 443-0414

#35
Sisters of the New South
Cuisines: Southern, Soul Food, Caterer
Average price: Inexpensive
Address: 2605 Skidaway Rd
Savannah, GA 31404
Phone: (912) 335-2761

#36
Wall's BBQ
Cuisines: Barbeque, Southern, Soul Food
Average price: Inexpensive
Address: 515 E York Ln
Savannah, GA 31401
Phone: (912) 232-9754

#37
Yia Yia Kitchen
Cuisines: Bakery, Greek
Average price: Inexpensive
Address: 3113 Habersham St
Savannah, GA 31405
Phone: (912) 200-3796

#38
Cafe M
Cuisines: Cafe, Breakfast & Brunch, French
Average price: Inexpensive
Address: 128 E Bay St
Savannah, GA 31401
Phone: (912) 712-3342

#39
Pie Society
Cuisines: Desserts, British, Bakery
Average price: Inexpensive
Address: 19 Jefferson St
Savannah, GA 31322
Phone: (912) 238-1144

#40
Randy's Bar Bq
Cuisines: Barbeque
Average price: Inexpensive
Address: 750 Wheaton St
Savannah, GA 31401
Phone: (912) 358-0701

#41
Huey's On The River
Cuisines: American
Average price: Modest
Address: 115 E River St
Savannah, GA 31401
Phone: (912) 232-3086

#42
Clary's Cafe
Cuisines: Breakfast & Brunch
Average price: Inexpensive
Address: 404 Abercorn St
Savannah, GA 31401
Phone: (912) 233-0402

#43
Jazz'D Tapas Bar
Cuisines: Jazz & Blues, Bar, Tapas Bar
Average price: Modest
Address: 52 Barnard St
Savannah, GA 31401
Phone: (912) 421-4310

#44
Savannah Filipino Authentic Cuisine
Cuisines: Filipino
Average price: Inexpensive
Address: 5515 Waters Ave
Savannah, GA 31404
Phone: (912) 201-3541

#45
Vic's On The River
Cuisines: Seafood, Southern
Average price: Expensive
Address: 26 E Bay St
Savannah, GA 31401
Phone: (912) 721-1000

#46
The Wyld Dock Bar
Cuisines: American, Seafood
Average price: Modest
Address: 2740 Livingston Ave
Savannah, GA 31406
Phone: (912) 692-1219

#47
Goose Feathers Cafe & Bakery
Cuisines: Sandwiches, Bakery
Average price: Inexpensive
Address: 39 Barnard St
Savannah, GA 31401
Phone: (912) 233-4683

#48
17Hundred90 Inn and Restaurant
Cuisines: American, Seafood, Burgers
Average price: Modest
Address: 307 E President St
Savannah, GA 31401
Phone: (912) 236-7122

#49
The Cotton Exchange
Seafood Grill & Tavern
Cuisines: American
Average price: Modest
Address: 201 E River St
Savannah, GA 31401
Phone: (912) 232-7088

#50
Henry's
Cuisines: Diner, Breakfast & Brunch
Average price: Inexpensive
Address: 28 Drayton St
Savannah, GA 31401
Phone: (912) 232-6628

#51
The District Cafe and Eatery
Cuisines: Cafe, Sandwiches
Average price: Inexpensive
Address: 202 E Broughton St
Savannah, GA 31401
Phone: (912) 443-0909

#52
Circa 1875
Cuisines: Pub, French
Average price: Expensive
Address: 48 Whitaker St
Savannah, GA 31401
Phone: (912) 443-1875

#53
The Pirate's House
Cuisines: Southern
Average price: Modest
Address: 20 E Broad St
Savannah, GA 31401
Phone: (912) 233-5757

#54
The Juicy Seafood
Cuisines: Seafood
Average price: Modest
Address: 7805 Abercorn St
Savannah, GA 31406
Phone: (912) 355-6658

#55
J Christopher's
Cuisines: American, Breakfast & Brunch
Average price: Modest
Address: 122 E Liberty St
Savannah, GA 31412
Phone: (912) 236-7494

#56
Seafoodlicious
Cuisines: Seafood Market,
Seafood, Fish & Chips
Average price: Inexpensive
Address: 4435 Skidaway Rd
Savannah, GA 31404
Phone: (912) 356-9988

#57
The Distillery
Cuisines: American, Pub, Gastropub
Average price: Modest
Address: 416 W Liberty St
Savannah, GA 31401
Phone: (912) 236-1772

#58
Our Daily Bread Cafe
Cuisines: Coffee & Tea, Bakery,
Breakfast & Brunch
Average price: Inexpensive
Address: 6 E State St
Savannah, GA 31401
Phone: (912) 713-4977

#59
Chiriya
Cuisines: Thai, Hawaiian
Average price: Modest
Address: 3017 E Victory Dr
Savannah, GA 31404
Phone: (912) 691-2080

#60
Soda Pop Shoppe
Cuisines: Sandwiches, Ice Cream, American
Average price: Inexpensive
Address: 114 Bull St
Savannah, GA 31401
Phone: (912) 236-5860

#61
The Noodle Bowl
Cuisines: Noodles, Salad, Soup
Average price: Modest
Address: 7054 Hodgson Memorial Dr
Savannah, GA 31406
Phone: (912) 692-1394

#62
Mirabelle Suites & Café
Cuisines: Cafe, Vacation Rentals
Average price: Inexpensive
Address: 313 Abercorn St
Savannah, GA 31401
Phone: (912) 335-7255

#63
Barracuda Bob's
Cuisines: Bar, Seafood
Average price: Modest
Address: 19 E River St
Savannah, GA 31401
Phone: (912) 330-6744

#64
Fire Street Food
Cuisines: Burgers, Vegan, Asian Fusion
Average price: Modest
Address: 13 E Perry St
Savannah, GA 31401
Phone: (912) 234-7776

#65
Vinnie Van Go-Go's
Cuisines: Pizza
Average price: Inexpensive
Address: 317 W Bryan St
Savannah, GA 31401
Phone: (912) 233-6394

#66
Zoës Kitchen
Cuisines: Mediterranean, Southern, Greek
Average price: Inexpensive
Address: 1821 E Victory Dr
Savannah, GA 31404
Phone: (912) 335-1375

#67
Sandfly BBQ
Cuisines: Barbeque
Average price: Modest
Address: 8413 Ferguson Ave
Savannah, GA 31406
Phone: (912) 356-5463

#68
Masada Cafe at the United House of Prayer
Cuisines: Southern
Average price: Inexpensive
Address: 2301 W Bay St
Savannah, GA 31412
Phone: (912) 236-9499

#69
Chive Sea Bar & Lounge
Cuisines: Seafood, Lounge
Average price: Modest
Address: 4 W Broughton Ln
Savannah, GA 31401
Phone: (912) 233-1748

#70
Screamin' Mimi's
Cuisines: Pizza
Average price: Inexpensive
Address: 513 E Oglethorpe Ave
Savannah, GA 31401
Phone: (912) 236-2744

#71
Soho South Cafe
Cuisines: American, Sandwiches
Average price: Modest
Address: 12 W Liberty St
Savannah, GA 31401
Phone: (912) 233-1633

#72
Noble Fare
Cuisines: American, French
Average price: Expensive
Address: 321 Jefferson St
Savannah, GA 31401
Phone: (912) 443-3210

#73
Bella Napoli Italian Bistro & Pizzeria
Cuisines: Italian, Pizza
Average price: Modest
Address: 18 E State St
Savannah, GA 31401
Phone: (912) 355-5555

#74
The Blue Door
Cuisines: Coffee & Tea,
Breakfast & Brunch, Sandwiches
Average price: Inexpensive
Address: 1718 Bull St
Savannah, GA 31401
Phone: (912) 335-1243

#75
The 5 Spot
Cuisines: American
Average price: Modest
Address: 4430 Habersham St
Savannah, GA 31405
Phone: (912) 777-3021

#76
Sorry Charlie's
Cuisines: Seafood
Average price: Modest
Address: 116 W Congress St
Savannah, GA 31401
Phone: (912) 234-5397

#77
A Lure Low Country Cuisine
Cuisines: Southern, American, Seafood
Average price: Expensive
Address: 309 W Congress St
Savannah, GA 31401
Phone: (912) 233-2111

#78
Kayak Kafé
Cuisines: Tex-Mex, Mexican, Sandwiches
Average price: Modest
Address: 1 E Broughton St
Savannah, GA 31401
Phone: (912) 233-6044

#79
Boomy's
Cuisines: Pub, Thai
Average price: Modest
Address: 409 W Congress St
Savannah, GA 31401
Phone: (912) 421-3162

#80
**Molly MacPherson's
Scottish Pub & Grill**
Cuisines: Pub, Scottish
Average price: Modest
Address: 311 W Congress St
Savannah, GA 31401
Phone: (912) 239-9600

#81
Rancho Alegre Cuban Restaurant
Cuisines: Cuban, Caribbean, Jazz & Blues
Average price: Modest
Address: 402 Martin Luther King
Junior Blvd, Savannah, GA 31401
Phone: (912) 292-1656

#82
Boar's Head Grill & Tavern
Cuisines: American
Average price: Modest
Address: 1 N Lincoln St
Savannah, GA 31401
Phone: (912) 651-9660

#83
Kayak Kafe
Cuisines: Mexican, Bar, Vegetarian
Average price: Modest
Address: 5002 Paulsen St
Savannah, GA 31405
Phone: (912) 349-4371

#84
Spudnik
Cuisines: Fast Food, Gluten-Free
Average price: Inexpensive
Address: 416 W Broughton St
Savannah, GA 31401
Phone: (912) 232-1986

#85
Hirano's
Cuisines: Japanese, Sushi Bar
Average price: Inexpensive
Address: 4426 Habersham St
Savannah, GA 31405
Phone: (912) 353-8337

#86
Tequila's Town
Cuisines: Mexican
Average price: Modest
Address: 109 Whitaker St
Savannah, GA 31401
Phone: (912) 236-3222

#87
Six Pence Pub
Cuisines: American, Pub
Average price: Modest
Address: 245 Bull St
Savannah, GA 31401
Phone: (912) 233-3151

#88
Smith Brother's Butcher Shop
Cuisines: Butcher, Meat Shop, Deli
Average price: Expensive
Address: 535 E Liberty St
Savannah, GA 31401
Phone: (912) 239-4512

#89
CO
Cuisines: Sushi Bar, Noodles
Average price: Modest
Address: 10 Whitaker St
Savannah, GA 31401
Phone: (912) 234-5375

#90
Butterhead Greens Cafe
Cuisines: Internet Cafe, Sandwiches
Average price: Inexpensive
Address: 1813 Bull St
Savannah, GA 31401
Phone: (912) 201-1808

#91
Chart House
Cuisines: Seafood, Steakhouse
Average price: Expensive
Address: 202 W Bay St
Savannah, GA 31401
Phone: (912) 234-6686

#92
Skyler's
Cuisines: American
Average price: Modest
Address: 225 E Bay St
Savannah, GA 31401
Phone: (912) 232-3955

#93
39 Rue de Jean
Cuisines: French, Brasseries
Average price: Expensive
Address: 605 W Oglethorpe Ave
Savannah, GA 31401
Phone: (912) 721-0595

#94
Blowin' Smoke
Cuisines: Mexican, Southern
Average price: Modest
Address: 1611 Habersham St
Savannah, GA 31401
Phone: (912) 231-2385

#95
River House Seafood
Cuisines: Seafood
Average price: Modest
Address: 125 W River St
Savannah, GA 31401
Phone: (912) 234-1900

#96
The Florence
Cuisines: Coffee & Tea, Italian, Cocktail Bar
Average price: Expensive
Address: 1 W Victory Dr
Savannah, GA 31405
Phone: (912) 234-5522

#97
Le Cafe Gourmet
Cuisines: Creperie, Bakery, Cafe
Average price: Inexpensive
Address: 53 Montgomery St
Savannah, GA 31401
Phone: (912) 200-3258

#98
The Bier Haus Gastropub
Cuisines: Belgian, German, Gastropub
Average price: Modest
Address: 513 E Oglethorpe Ave
Savannah, GA 31401
Phone: (912) 349-1163

#99
45 Bistro
Cuisines: French, Bar, Venue & Event Space
Average price: Expensive
Address: 123 E Broughton St
Savannah, GA 31401
Phone: (912) 234-3111

#100
Pacci Italian Kitchen + Bar
Cuisines: Italian
Average price: Modest
Address: 601 E Bay St
Savannah, GA 31401
Phone: (912) 233-6002

#101
Al Salaam Deli
Cuisines: Middle Eastern
Average price: Inexpensive
Address: 2311 Habersham St
Savannah, GA 31401
Phone: (912) 447-0400

#102
Wet Willie's
Cuisines: Bar, American
Average price: Inexpensive
Address: 101 E River St
Savannah, GA 31401
Phone: (912) 233-5650

#103
Troy Mediterranean Cuisine
Cuisines: Greek, Mediterranean
Average price: Modest
Address: 10510 Abercorn St
Savannah, GA 31419
Phone: (912) 921-5117

#104
The Chromatic Dragon
Cuisines: American, Pub
Average price: Modest
Address: 514 MLK Jr Blvd
Savannah, GA 31401
Phone: (912) 289-0350

#105
The Lady & Sons
Cuisines: Southern, American
Average price: Modest
Address: 102 W Congress St
Savannah, GA 31401
Phone: (912) 233-2600

#106
Antojo Latino
Cuisines: Latin American
Average price: Modest
Address: 44 Posey St
Savannah, GA 31406
Phone: (912) 224-9282

#107
The Firefly
Cuisines: Desserts, Sandwiches, Salad
Average price: Modest
Address: 321 Habersham St
Savannah, GA 31401
Phone: (912) 234-1971

#108
Barberitos
Cuisines: Tex-Mex
Average price: Inexpensive
Address: 4525 Habersham St
Savannah, GA 31405
Phone: (912) 349-6750

#109
Roly Poly
Cuisines: Fast Food
Average price: Inexpensive
Address: 114 Barnard St
Savannah, GA 31401
Phone: (912) 233-8222

#110
Caribbean Cuisine Restaurant
Cuisines: Caribbean
Average price: Modest
Address: 7094 Hodgson Memorial Dr
Savannah, GA 31406
Phone: (912) 335-7629

#111
Hao Mongolian Grill
Cuisines: Mongolian
Average price: Modest
Address: 7312 Hodgson Memorial Dr
Savannah, GA 31406
Phone: (912) 777-7596

#112
Ben's Neighborhood Grill & TAP
Cuisines: Pub, Greek, American
Average price: Modest
Address: 7080 Hodgson Memorial Dr
Savannah, GA 31406
Phone: (912) 351-9008

#113
Moon River Brewing Company
Cuisines: Pub, Brewery, American
Average price: Modest
Address: 21 W Bay St
Savannah, GA 31401
Phone: (912) 447-0943

#114
Panaderia La Canasta
Cuisines: Mexican
Average price: Inexpensive
Address: 1545 East Montgomery X Rd
Savannah, GA 31406
Phone: (912) 352-4800

#115
Pearl's Saltwater Grille
Cuisines: American
Average price: Modest
Address: 7000 La Roche Ave
Savannah, GA 31406
Phone: (912) 352-8221

#116
Five Oaks Taproom
Cuisines: American, Beer, Wine & Spirits
Average price: Modest
Address: 201 W Bay St
Savannah, GA 31401
Phone: (912) 236-4440

#117
Driftaway Cafe
Cuisines: American, Seafood
Average price: Modest
Address: 7400 Skidaway Rd
Savannah, GA 31406
Phone: (912) 303-0999

#118
La Parrilla Mexican Restaurant
Cuisines: Mexican
Average price: Modest
Address: 7804 Abercorn Extension
Savannah, GA 31406
Phone: (912) 354-3757

#119
Lil Chick
Cuisines: Southern
Average price: Inexpensive
Address: 2901 W Bay St
Savannah, GA 31408
Phone: (912) 964-6350

#120
The Shrimp Factory
Cuisines: Seafood
Average price: Modest
Address: 313 E River St
Savannah, GA 31401
Phone: (912) 236-4229

#121
**Mansion on Forsyth Park
Autograph Collection**
Cuisines: Hotels, American
Average price: Expensive
Address: 700 Drayton St.
Savannah, GA 31401
Phone: (912) 238-5158

#122
Bonefish Grill
Cuisines: Seafood
Average price: Modest
Address: 5500 Abercorn St
Savannah, GA 31405
Phone: (912) 691-2575

#123
Sapphire Grill
Cuisines: American
Average price: Expensive
Address: 110 W Congress St
Savannah, GA 31401
Phone: (912) 443-9962

#124
The Warehouse
Cuisines: American, Bar
Average price: Inexpensive
Address: 18 E River St
Savannah, GA 31401
Phone: (912) 234-6003

#125
Sentient Bean
Cuisines: Coffee & Tea, Vegan, Vegetarian
Average price: Inexpensive
Address: 13 E Park Ave
Savannah, GA 31401
Phone: (912) 232-4447

#126
B&D Burgers
Cuisines: American, Burgers
Average price: Modest
Address: 209 W Congress St
Savannah, GA 31401
Phone: (912) 238-8315

#127
Island Breeze
Cuisines: Caribbean
Average price: Inexpensive
Address: 2818 Montgomery St
Savannah, GA 31405
Phone: (912) 233-7300

#128
**Belford's Savannah
Seafood & Steaks**
Cuisines: Steakhouse, Southern
Average price: Expensive
Address: 315 W Saint Julian St
Savannah, GA 31401
Phone: (912) 233-2626

#129
Latin Chicks
Cuisines: Latin American
Average price: Inexpensive
Address: 5205 Waters Ave
Savannah, GA 31404
Phone: (912) 495-5133

#130
Wiley's Championship BBQ
Cuisines: Barbeque
Average price: Modest
Address: 4700 Hwy 80 E
Savannah, GA 31410
Phone: (912) 201-3259

#131
Your Pie
Cuisines: Pizza, Salad, Italian
Average price: Inexpensive
Address: 110 W Bryan St
Savannah, GA 31401
Phone: (912) 234-2433

#132
Leopold's Ice Cream
Cuisines: Ice Cream, Sandwiches,
Coffee & Tea
Average price: Inexpensive
Address: 212 E Broughton St
Savannah, GA 31401
Phone: (912) 234-4442

#133
5-Twenty Wings
Cuisines: Chicken Wings
Average price: Inexpensive
Address: 2705 Bull St
Savannah, GA 31401
Phone: (912) 349-5317

#134
Rocks on the River
Cuisines: American, Comfort Food
Average price: Modest
Address: 102 W Bay St
Savannah, GA 31401
Phone: (912) 721-3800

#135
City Market
Cuisines: Art Gallery, Fast Food
Average price: Modest
Address: 219 W Bryan St
Savannah, GA 31401
Phone: (912) 232-4903

#136
B's Cracklin' BBQ
Cuisines: Barbeque
Average price: Modest
Address: 12409 White Bluff Rd
Savannah, GA 31419
Phone: (912) 330-6921

#137
Savannah Taphouse
Cuisines: Sports Bar, Burgers, American
Average price: Modest
Address: 125 E. Broughton St.
Savannah, GA 31401
Phone: (912) 201-8277

#138
The Funky Brunch Cafe
Cuisines: Breakfast & Brunch, Cafe
Average price: Modest
Address: 304 E Broughton St
Savannah, GA 31401
Phone: (912) 234-3050

#139
Putt Guttz
Cuisines: Desserts, Deli
Average price: Modest
Address: 714 MLK Jr Blvd
Savannah, GA 31401
Phone: (912) 349-4338

#140
Garibaldi's Cafe
Cuisines: Italian, Cafe, Seafood
Average price: Expensive
Address: 315 W Congress St
Savannah, GA 31401
Phone: (912) 232-7118

#141
Corleone's Trattoria
Cuisines: Italian
Average price: Modest
Address: 44 Martin Luther King Blvd
Savannah, GA 31401
Phone: (912) 232-2720

#142
Wright Square Cafe
Cuisines: Sandwiches
Average price: Inexpensive
Address: 21 W York St
Savannah, GA 31401
Phone: (912) 238-1150

#143
Sunny Side Up
Cuisines: Breakfast & Brunch
Average price: Inexpensive
Address: 800 E DE Renne Ave
Savannah, GA 31405
Phone: (912) 354-2289

#144
Tijuana Flats
Cuisines: Tex-Mex, Mexican
Average price: Inexpensive
Address: 1800 East Victory Dr
Savannah, GA 31404
Phone: (912) 344-9111

#145
Savannah Coffee Roasters
Cuisines: Cafe, Bakery
Average price: Inexpensive
Address: 215 W Liberty St
Savannah, GA 31401
Phone: (912) 352-2994

#146
Jason's Deli
Cuisines: American
Average price: Inexpensive
Address: 318 Mall Blvd
Savannah, GA 31406
Phone: (912) 355-7955

#147
Windsor Cafeteria
Cuisines: Southern, Breakfast & Brunch
Average price: Inexpensive
Address: 12313 Largo Dr
Savannah, GA 31419
Phone: (912) 925-6103

#148
Sakura Buffet
Cuisines: Buffet
Average price: Modest
Address: 220 Eisenhower Dr
Savannah, GA 31406
Phone: (912) 352-9668

#149
Cohen's Retreat
Cuisines: American, Art Gallery
Average price: Expensive
Address: 5715 Skidaway Rd
Savannah, GA 31406
Phone: (912) 355-3336

#150
Laurie's Restaurant
Cuisines: American
Average price: Inexpensive
Address: 10 W State St
Savannah, GA 31401
Phone: (912) 236-3322

#151
Savannah's World Famous Shave Ice
Cuisines: Ice Cream, Sandwiches,
Shaved Ice
Average price: Inexpensive
Address: 214 W Boundary St
Savannah, GA 31401
Phone: (912) 200-4252

#152
Fiddler's Crab House
Cuisines: Seafood Market, Seafood
Average price: Modest
Address: 131 W River St
Savannah, GA 31401
Phone: (912) 644-7172

#153
Rocks on the Roof
Cuisines: American, Cocktail Bar
Average price: Modest
Address: 102 W Bay St
Savannah, GA 31401
Phone: (912) 721-3901

#154
Tubby's Tank House
Cuisines: Seafood, Bar
Average price: Modest
Address: 2909 River Dr
Savannah, GA 31404
Phone: (912) 354-9040

#155
Churchill's Pub
Cuisines: Pub, British, Vegetarian
Average price: Modest
Address: 13 W Bay St
Savannah, GA 31401
Phone: (912) 232-8501

#156
Fiore Italian Bar & Grill
Cuisines: Italian, Bar
Average price: Modest
Address: 7360 Skidaway Rd
Savannah, GA 31406
Phone: (912) 349-2609

#157
Sweet Melissa's
Cuisines: Pizza
Average price: Inexpensive
Address: 103 W Congress St
Savannah, GA 31401
Phone: (912) 341-0093

#158
Savannah Smiles Dueling Pianos
Cuisines: Bar, American, Piano Bar
Average price: Modest
Address: 314 Williamson St
Savannah, GA 31401
Phone: (912) 527-6453

#159
The Naked Dog
Cuisines: Street Vendors, Hot Dogs
Average price: Inexpensive
Address: 502 E River St
Savannah, GA 31401
Phone: (912) 777-9555

#160
Bernie's River Street
Cuisines: Seafood
Average price: Modest
Address: 115 E River St
Savannah, GA 31401
Phone: (912) 236-1827

#161
Peggy Lynn's Country Cooking
Cuisines: Southern
Average price: Inexpensive
Address: 4119 Ogeechee Rd
Savannah, GA 31405
Phone: (912) 447-8434

#162
Puerto Rico Restaurant
Cuisines: Latin American
Average price: Modest
Address: 310 E Montgomery Cross Rd
Savannah, GA 31406
Phone: (912) 224-4017

#163
Bella's Italian Cafe
Cuisines: Italian, Pizza, Wine Bar
Average price: Modest
Address: 4420 Habersham St
Savannah, GA 31405
Phone: (912) 354-4005

#164
Korea Garden
Cuisines: Korean, Barbeque
Average price: Modest
Address: 20 E Derenne Ave
Savannah, GA 31405
Phone: (912) 201-1771

#165
Green Tea Restaurant
Cuisines: Chinese
Average price: Inexpensive
Address: 7205 Waters Ave
Savannah, GA 31406
Phone: (912) 691-0330

#166
Russo's Seafood
Cuisines: Seafood
Average price: Inexpensive
Address: 209 E 40th St
Savannah, GA 31401
Phone: (912) 421-6432

#167
McDonough's
Cuisines: Pub, American
Average price: Inexpensive
Address: 21 E McDonough St
Savannah, GA 31401
Phone: (912) 233-6136

#168
Chicken Salad Chick
Cuisines: Salad, Sandwiches, Deli
Average price: Inexpensive
Address: 7400 Abercorn St
Savannah, GA 31406
Phone: (912) 200-5286

#169
The Bayou Cafe
Cuisines: Cafe, American, Seafood
Average price: Modest
Address: 14 N Abercorn Ramp
Savannah, GA 31401
Phone: (912) 233-6411

#170
Savannah Fried Chicken
Cuisines: Chicken Wings
Average price: Inexpensive
Address: 2108 Bona Bella Ave
Savannah, GA 31406
Phone: (912) 352-2205

#171
Cha-Bella
Cuisines: American
Average price: Expensive
Address: 102 E Broad St
Savannah, GA 31401
Phone: (912) 790-7888

#172
The Naked Dog
& Reality Bites Bakery
Cuisines: Hot Dogs, Donuts
Average price: Modest
Address: 1514 Bull St
Savannah, GA 31401
Phone: (912) 344-4828

#173
Tubby's Seafood River Street
Cuisines: Seafood
Average price: Modest
Address: 115 E River St
Savannah, GA 31401
Phone: (912) 233-0770

#174
Pakwan Indian Cuisine
Cuisines: Indian
Average price: Modest
Address: 7102 Abercorn St
Savannah, GA 31406
Phone: (912) 349-4261

#175
Fiddler's Seafood
Cuisines: Seafood, Bar
Average price: Modest
Address: 7201 Hodgson Memorial Dr
Savannah, GA 31406
Phone: (912) 351-2274

#176
Russo's Seafood
Cuisines: Seafood
Average price: Modest
Address: 201 E 40th St
Savannah, GA 31401
Phone: (912) 234-5196

#177
JJ Bonerz
Cuisines: Bar, American, Pizza
Average price: Modest
Address: 11 W Bay St
Savannah, GA 31401
Phone: (912) 944-4343

#178
Saddle Bags
Cuisines: Southern, Sports Bar, Pool Hall
Average price: Inexpensive
Address: 317 W River St
Savannah, GA 31401
Phone: (912) 349-5275

#179
Wild Wing Cafe
Cuisines: Sports Bar, American
Average price: Modest
Address: 27 Barnard St
Savannah, GA 31401
Phone: (912) 790-9464

#180
PJ Thai Cuisine
Cuisines: Thai, American
Average price: Modest
Address: 147 Abercorn St
Savannah, GA 31401
Phone: (912) 201-3534

#181
The Melting Pot
Cuisines: Fondue, American
Average price: Expensive
Address: 232 E Broughton St
Savannah, GA 31401
Phone: (912) 349-5676

#182
Saigon Bistro
Cuisines: Vietnamese, Asian Fusion
Average price: Inexpensive
Address: 5700 Waters Ave
Savannah, GA 31404
Phone: (912) 335-2025

#183
Mellow Mushroom
Cuisines: Pizza, Bar, Sandwiches
Average price: Modest
Address: 11 W Liberty St
Savannah, GA 31401
Phone: (912) 495-0705

#184
B&D Burgers
Cuisines: Burgers
Average price: Modest
Address: 13 E Broughton St
Savannah, GA 31401
Phone: (912) 231-0986

#185
Lili's Restaurant and Bar
Cuisines: Seafood, French, Asian Fusion
Average price: Modest
Address: 326 Johnny Mercer Blvd
Savannah, GA 31410
Phone: (912) 235-2664

#186
Aqua Star
Cuisines: Seafood, Breakfast & Brunch
Average price: Expensive
Address: 1 Resort Dr
Savannah, GA 31421
Phone: (912) 201-2085

#187
Lizzy's Tequila Bar & Grill
Cuisines: American, Seafood, Mexican
Average price: Modest
Address: 417 E River St
Savannah, GA 31401
Phone: (912) 341-8897

#188
Kimchi 2 Restaurant
Cuisines: Korean
Average price: Modest
Address: 149 E Montgomery Cross Rd
Savannah, GA 31406
Phone: (912) 227-2025

#189
Congress Street Social Club
Cuisines: American, Burgers
Average price: Inexpensive
Address: 411 W Congress St
Savannah, GA 31401
Phone: (912) 238-1985

#190
Yohane
Cuisines: Japanese, Korean
Average price: Modest
Address: 7084 Hodgson Memorial Dr
Savannah, GA 31406
Phone: (912) 355-8876

#191
Sunrise Restaurant
Cuisines: Breakfast & Brunch, American
Average price: Inexpensive
Address: 1 Southern Oaks Ct
Savannah, GA 31405
Phone: (912) 238-8018

#192
Nicky's Pizzeria
Cuisines: Pizza, Italian, Sandwiches
Average price: Inexpensive
Address: 2 Park of Commerce Dr
Savannah, GA 31405
Phone: (912) 358-0248

#193
Coffee Deli
Cuisines: Deli, Coffee & Tea
Average price: Inexpensive
Address: 4517 Habersham St
Savannah, GA 31405
Phone: (912) 352-7818

#194
FULL Lunch and Late Night
Cuisines: Cajun/Creole, Burgers, Hot Dogs
Average price: Inexpensive
Address: 35 Whitaker St
Savannah, GA 31401
Phone: (912) 712-5150

#195
Tangerine Fusion + Sushi Bar
Cuisines: Sushi Bar, Thai
Average price: Modest
Address: 11215 Abercorn St
Savannah, GA 31419
Phone: (912) 920-5504

#196
Lucky's Market
Cuisines: Grocery, Deli, Sandwiches
Average price: Modest
Address: 5501 Abercorn St
Savannah, GA 31405
Phone: (912) 349-5369

#197
The Howlin Hound
Cuisines: American, Burgers, Sandwiches
Average price: Modest
Address: 6730 Waters Ave
Savannah, GA 31406
Phone: (912) 777-4717

#198
The King & I
Cuisines: Thai
Average price: Modest
Address: 7098 Hodgson Memorial Dr
Savannah, GA 31406
Phone: (912) 355-2100

#199
Stoner's Pizza Joint
Cuisines: Pizza
Average price: Inexpensive
Address: 1100 Eisenhower Dr
Savannah, GA 31406
Phone: (912) 495-5372

#200
Olympia Cafe
Cuisines: Greek
Average price: Modest
Address: 5 E River St
Savannah, GA 31401
Phone: (912) 233-3131

#201
Dockside Seafood
Cuisines: Seafood
Average price: Modest
Address: 201 W River St
Savannah, GA 31401
Phone: (912) 233-3810

#202
Ole Times Country Buffet
Cuisines: Buffet
Average price: Modest
Address: 209 Stephenson Ave
Savannah, GA 31405
Phone: (912) 356-1630

#203
Top Deck
Cuisines: American, Tapas, Cocktail Bar
Average price: Modest
Address: 125 W River St
Savannah, GA 31401
Phone: (912) 436-6828

#204
Ronnie's Restaurant
Cuisines: Burgers
Average price: Inexpensive
Address: 1501 Dean Forest Rd
Savannah, GA 31408
Phone: (912) 964-8465

#205
Mabel's Cupcake Emporium
Cuisines: Cupcakes, Breakfast & Brunch
Average price: Inexpensive
Address: 151 W Bryan St
Savannah, GA 31401
Phone: (912) 341-8014

#206
Text to table
Cuisines: Soul Food, Sandwiches
Average price: Inexpensive
Address: 43 Whitaker St
Savannah, GA 31401
Phone: (912) 247-1591

#207
Carlito's Mexican Bar and Grill
Cuisines: Mexican
Average price: Modest
Address: 119 Martin Luther King Jr Blvd
Savannah, GA 31401
Phone: (912) 232-2525

#208
Tailgate Sports Bar & Grill
Cuisines: Sports Bar, American
Average price: Modest
Address: 11215 Abercorn St
Savannah, GA 31419
Phone: (912) 921-2269

#209
Star Kitchen Chinese Restaurant
Cuisines: Chinese
Average price: Inexpensive
Address: 2504 Skidaway Rd
Savannah, GA 31404
Phone: (912) 201-3028

#210
The Wormhole Music Club and Bar
Cuisines: Music Venue, Dive Bar, American
Average price: Inexpensive
Address: 2307 Bull St
Savannah, GA 31401
Phone: (912) 349-6770

#211
Bar.Food
Cuisines: Wine Bar, American
Average price: Modest
Address: 4523 Habersham St
Savannah, GA 31405
Phone: (912) 355-5956

#212
Hop Xing Chinese Restaurant
Cuisines: Chinese, Soup, Buffet
Average price: Inexpensive
Address: 1900 E Victory Dr
Savannah, GA 31404
Phone: (912) 234-1101

#213
Shabazz Seafood Restaurant
Cuisines: Seafood
Average price: Modest
Address: 502 W Victory Dr
Savannah, GA 31405
Phone: (912) 236-7477

#214
Spanky's Pizza Galley & Saloon
Cuisines: Burgers, Pizza, Sandwiches
Average price: Modest
Address: 317 E River St
Savannah, GA 31401
Phone: (912) 236-3009

#215
Allyanna's Olde Style Pizzeria
Cuisines: Pizza
Average price: Inexpensive
Address: 205-C E Montgomery Crossroads
Savannah, GA 31406
Phone: (912) 920-9099

#216
El Paso
Cuisines: Mexican, Tex-Mex
Average price: Modest
Address: 7921 Abercorn St
Savannah, GA 31416
Phone: (912) 927-2354

#217
Munchie's BBQ & SUBS
Cuisines: Barbeque
Average price: Inexpensive
Address: 2110 Montgomery St
Savannah, GA 31401
Phone: (912) 335-1118

#218
Midtown Deli & Bagel Shop
Cuisines: Bagels, American
Average price: Inexpensive
Address: 7805 Abercorn St
Savannah, GA 31406
Phone: (912) 417-6810

#219
Kanpai 2
Cuisines: Japanese
Average price: Modest
Address: 2 Park of Commerce Blvd
Savannah, GA 31405
Phone: (912) 231-8282

#220
Loc's Chicken & Waffles
Cuisines: Breakfast & Brunch, Sandwiches
Average price: Inexpensive
Address: 7360 Skidaway Rd
Savannah, GA 31406
Phone: (912) 692-1114

#221
700 Drayton Restaurant
Cuisines: American
Average price: Expensive
Address: 700 Drayton St
Savannah, GA 31401
Phone: (912) 721-5002

#222
Five Guys Burgers and Fries
Cuisines: Burgers, Fast Food
Average price: Inexpensive
Address: 175 W Bay St
Savannah, GA 31401
Phone: (912) 238-1227

#223
Billy's Place at McDonough's
Cuisines: American
Average price: Modest
Address: 21 E Perry St
Savannah, GA 31401
Phone: (912) 231-9049

#224
Paula Deen's Restaurant
Cuisines: American
Average price: Modest
Address: 102 W Congress St
Savannah, GA 31401
Phone: (912) 233-2600

#225
Unforgettable Bakery & Deli
Cuisines: Deli, Bakery, Sandwiches
Average price: Modest
Address: 238 Eisenhower Dr
Savannah, GA 31406
Phone: (912) 355-6160

#226
Forsyth Park Cafe
Cuisines: Cafe
Average price: Inexpensive
Address: 621 Drayton St
Savannah, GA 31401
Phone: (912) 233-7848

#227
China Wok
Cuisines: Chinese
Average price: Inexpensive
Address: 821 King George Blvd
Savannah, GA 31419
Phone: (912) 927-0886

#228
Sushi Zen
Cuisines: Sushi Bar, Japanese
Average price: Modest
Address: 1100 Eisenhower Dr
Savannah, GA 31406
Phone: (912) 303-0141

#229
Asian River
Cuisines: Asian Fusion
Average price: Modest
Address: 1100 Eisenhower Dr
Savannah, GA 31406
Phone: (912) 354-6111

#230
Larry's Restaurant
Cuisines: American
Average price: Inexpensive
Address: 3000 Skidaway Rd
Savannah, GA 31404
Phone: (912) 355-5821

#231
Whistle Stop Cafe
Cuisines: American
Average price: Inexpensive
Address: 303 Martin Luther King Jr Blvd
Savannah, GA 31401
Phone: (912) 651-3656

#232
Coach's Corner
Cuisines: Sports Bar, American
Average price: Modest
Address: 3016 E Victory Dr
Savannah, GA 31404
Phone: (912) 352-2933

#233
China Taste
Cuisines: Chinese
Average price: Inexpensive
Address: 2208 E Derenne Ave
Savannah, GA 31406
Phone: (912) 335-1165

#234
Kakki Restaurant
Cuisines: Japanese
Average price: Modest
Address: 4700 US Hwy 80 E
Savannah, GA 31410
Phone: (912) 898-3880

#235
Beetnix Savannah Juice Bar
Cuisines: Vegan, Juice Bar, Salad
Average price: Modest
Address: 18 E Broughton St
Savannah, GA 31401
Phone: (912) 231-9643

#236
Omelette House
Cuisines: Breakfast & Brunch
Average price: Inexpensive
Address: 7129 Hodgson Memorial Dr
Savannah, GA 31406
Phone: (912) 356-3388

#237
World Of Beer
Cuisines: Pub, American
Average price: Modest
Address: 112 W Broughton St
Savannah, GA 31401
Phone: (912) 443-1515

#238
Joe's Crab Shack
Cuisines: Seafood, American
Average price: Modest
Address: 504 E River St
Savannah, GA 31401
Phone: (912) 232-1830

#239
Lisa's Chinese Take-Out
Cuisines: Chinese
Average price: Inexpensive
Address: 2315 Waters Ave
Savannah, GA 31404
Phone: (912) 236-8228

#240
Toni Steakhouse
Cuisines: Steakhouse
Average price: Modest
Address: 110 Eisenhower Dr
Savannah, GA 31406
Phone: (912) 691-8748

#241
Texas Roadhouse
Cuisines: Steakhouse, Barbeque, American
Average price: Modest
Address: 14045 Abercorn St
Savannah, GA 31419
Phone: (912) 961-5650

#242
Barnes Restaurant
Cuisines: Barbeque, Seafood, Sandwiches
Average price: Modest
Address: 5320 Waters Ave
Savannah, GA 31404
Phone: (912) 354-8745

#243
Five Guys Burgers and Fries
Cuisines: Burgers, Fast Food
Average price: Modest
Address: 5500 Abercorn St
Savannah, GA 31405
Phone: (912) 692-1161

#244
Mi Vida Loca
Cuisines: Mexican
Average price: Inexpensive
Address: 143 E Montgomery Xrd
Savannah, GA 31406
Phone: (912) 961-1488

#245
Spanky's Pizza Galley & Saloon
Cuisines: Pizza, Burgers, American
Average price: Modest
Address: 308 Mall Way
Savannah, GA 31406
Phone: (912) 355-3383

#246
Carey Hilliard's Restaurant
Cuisines: Seafood Market, Barbeque
Average price: Modest
Address: 3316 Skidaway Rd
Savannah, GA 31404
Phone: (912) 354-7240

#247
Chipotle Mexican Grill
Cuisines: Mexican, Fast Food
Average price: Inexpensive
Address: 1801 E Victory Dr
Savannah, GA 31404
Phone: (912) 303-5870

#248
Windows Restaurant
Cuisines: Breakfast & Brunch
Average price: Modest
Address: 2 W Bay St
Savannah, GA 31401
Phone: (912) 238-1234

#249
Bojangles
Cuisines: Fast Food
Average price: Inexpensive
Address: 29 W Derenne Ave
Savannah, GA 31405
Phone: (912) 353-7787

#250
The Original Pancake House
Cuisines: American, Sandwiches
Average price: Modest
Address: 7201 Hodgson Memorial Dr
Savannah, GA 31406
Phone: (912) 351-9333

#251
Peking House Restaurant
Cuisines: Chinese
Average price: Inexpensive
Address: 1216 Abercorn St
Savannah, GA 31401
Phone: (912) 238-8328

#252
K'Bella Gourmet Carry Out
Cuisines: American
Average price: Modest
Address: 119 Charlotte Dr
Savannah, GA 31410
Phone: (912) 897-4026

#253
Miyabi
Cuisines: Japanese
Average price: Modest
Address: 200 Eisenhower Dr
Savannah, GA 31406
Phone: (912) 352-7300

#254
Papa's Bar-B-Que & Seafood
Cuisines: Barbeque, Seafood
Average price: Modest
Address: 119 A Charlotte Rd
Savannah, GA 31410
Phone: (912) 897-0236

#255
Carrabba's Italian Grill
Cuisines: Italian, Seafood
Average price: Modest
Address: 10408 Abercorn St
Savannah, GA 31419
Phone: (912) 961-7073

#256
Nine Drayton
Cuisines: American
Average price: Modest
Address: 9 Drayton St
Savannah, GA 31401
Phone: (912) 443-1554

#257
Jackie's Seafood Market
Cuisines: Seafood
Average price: Modest
Address: 1117 E Montgomery Cross Rd
Savannah, GA 31406
Phone: (912) 927-2266

#258
Sushi-Zen Downtown
Cuisines: Sushi Bar, Japanese
Average price: Modest
Address: 30 Martin Luther King Jr Blvd
Savannah, GA 31401
Phone: (912) 233-1187

#259
Wayback Burgers
Cuisines: Burgers
Average price: Modest
Address: 8108 Abercorn St
Savannah, GA 31406
Phone: (912) 925-7654

#260
Jalapenos Mexican Grill
Cuisines: Mexican
Average price: Inexpensive
Address: 7405 Skidaway Rd
Savannah, GA 31406
Phone: (912) 356-1800

#261
Egg Roll King
Cuisines: Chinese
Average price: Inexpensive
Address: 1314 Montgomery St
Savannah, GA 31401
Phone: (912) 447-6833

#262
Little Italy Neighborhood Restaurant
Cuisines: Pizza, Italian, Wine Bar
Average price: Modest
Address: 138 Johnny Mercer Blvd
Savannah, GA 31410
Phone: (912) 201-3805

#263
Dickey's Barbecue Pit
Cuisines: Barbeque
Average price: Modest
Address: 13051 Abercorn Street
Savannah, GA 31419
Phone: (912) 200-3677

#264
Cook Out Savannah
Cuisines: Burgers
Average price: Inexpensive
Address: 11700 Abercorn St
Savannah, GA 31419
Phone: (912) 961-4441

#265
Ta Ca Sushi & Japanese Fusion
Cuisines: Sushi Bar, Japanese
Average price: Modest
Address: 513 E Oglethorp Ave
Savannah, GA 31401
Phone: (912) 232-8222

#266
Mandarin Wok
Cuisines: Chinese
Average price: Inexpensive
Address: 1 Diamond Cswy
Savannah, GA 31406
Phone: (912) 352-9999

#267
Carey Hilliard's Restaurant
Cuisines: American
Average price: Modest
Address: 8410 Waters Ave
Savannah, GA 31406
Phone: (912) 355-2468

#268
Carey Hilliard's Restaurant
Cuisines: Barbeque, Seafood, American
Average price: Modest
Address: 11111 Abercorn St
Savannah, GA 31419
Phone: (912) 925-3225

#269
La Comarca
Cuisines: Mexican
Average price: Inexpensive
Address: 4811 Ogeechee Rd
Savannah, GA 31405
Phone: (912) 401-0039

#270
Asian River
Cuisines: Chinese
Average price: Modest
Address: 20 E Derenne Ave
Savannah, GA 31405
Phone: (912) 239-4266

#271
A Taste Of Heaven Diner's Delight
Cuisines: Diner
Average price: Inexpensive
Address: 7010 Skidaway Rd
Savannah, GA 31406
Phone: (912) 349-2074

#272
Baldinos Giant Jersey Subs
Cuisines: Sandwiches, Salad, Steakhouse
Average price: Inexpensive
Address: 6600 White Bluff Rd
Savannah, GA 31405
Phone: (912) 352-7827

#273
Cancun Mexican Restaurant
Cuisines: Mexican
Average price: Inexpensive
Address: 5500 Abercorn St
Savannah, GA 31405
Phone: (912) 356-1333

#274
Cafe At City Market
Cuisines: Italian, Sandwiches, Cajun/Creole
Average price: Modest
Address: 224 W Saint Julian St
Savannah, GA 31401
Phone: (912) 236-7133

#275
Joe Loves Lobster Rolls
Cuisines: Seafood
Average price: Modest
Address: 111 Jazie Dr
Savannah, GA 31410
Phone: (912) 777-5937

#276
B&D Burgers
Cuisines: Burgers
Average price: Modest
Address: 11108 Abercorn St
Savannah, GA 31419
Phone: (912) 927-8700

#277
Chipotle Mexican Grill
Cuisines: Mexican, Fast Food
Average price: Inexpensive
Address: 318 Mall Blvd
Savannah, GA 31406
Phone: (912) 335-3380

#278
Bamboo Garden
Cuisines: Fast Food, Chinese
Average price: Inexpensive
Address: 13051 Abercorn St
Savannah, GA 31419
Phone: (912) 927-9668

#279
Garden City BBQ
Cuisines: Barbeque
Average price: Modest
Address: 4608 Augusta Rd
Savannah, GA 31408
Phone: (912) 349-3359

#280
Your Pie
Cuisines: Pizza, Salad, Italian
Average price: Modest
Address: 7360 Skidaway Rd
Savannah, GA 31406
Phone: (912) 692-1123

#281
Wang's II Chinese Restaurant
Cuisines: Chinese
Average price: Modest
Address: 7601 Waters Ave
Savannah, GA 31406
Phone: (912) 355-0321

#282
Ma Hanna's Chicken & Waffles
Cuisines: Southern
Average price: Inexpensive
Address: 724 W Oglethorpe
Savannah, GA 31401
Phone: (912) 234-2524

#283
Vincenzo's Pizzeria
Cuisines: Pizza
Average price: Modest
Address: 12417 White Bluff Rd
Savannah, GA 31419
Phone: (912) 921-7800

#284
Riverboat Pizza Company
Cuisines: Pizza
Average price: Modest
Address: 5975 Ogeechee Rd
Savannah, GA 31419
Phone: (912) 662-5074

#285
Jet's Pizza
Cuisines: Pizza
Average price: Inexpensive
Address: 7929 Abercorn St
Savannah, GA 31406
Phone: (912) 961-5387

#286
Sakura Japanese Restaurant
Cuisines: Japanese
Average price: Inexpensive
Address: 8465 Waters Ave
Savannah, GA 31406
Phone: (912) 351-9300

#287
Great Harvest Bread Company
Cuisines: Bakery, Salad, Sandwiches
Average price: Inexpensive
Address: 7360 Skidaway Rd
Savannah, GA 31406
Phone: (912) 777-7263

#288
Seasons Cafe
Cuisines: Sushi Bar, Japanese
Average price: Inexpensive
Address: 10 Barnard St
Savannah, GA 31401
Phone: (912) 349-6230

#289
John Ryan's Bistro
Cuisines: American
Average price: Modest
Address: 411 W Bay St
Savannah, GA 31401
Phone: (912) 790-7000

#290
Wasabi's Downtown
Cuisines: Japanese, Sushi Bar, Asian Fusion
Average price: Modest
Address: 113 Martin Luther King Blvd
Savannah, GA 31401
Phone: (912) 233-8899

#291
Zaxby's Chicken Fingers
& Buffalo Wings
Cuisines: Fast Food, Chicken Wings, Salad
Average price: Inexpensive
Address: 1917 E Victory Dr
Savannah, GA 31404
Phone: (912) 691-4722

#292
Mr Pizza
Cuisines: Pizza
Average price: Modest
Address: 2 Quacco Rd
Savannah, GA 31419
Phone: (912) 920-8951

#293
IHOP
Cuisines: American, Breakfast & Brunch
Average price: Inexpensive
Address: 1800 E Victory Dr
Savannah, GA 31404
Phone: (912) 233-6455

#294
17 Sakura
Cuisines: Japanese
Average price: Modest
Address: 5730 Ogeechee Rd
Savannah, GA 31405
Phone: (912) 234-7888

#295
Delicious Teriyaki Express
Cuisines: Japanese
Average price: Modest
Address: 1915 E Victory Dr
Savannah, GA 31404
Phone: (912) 401-0676

#296
Chinatown Buffet
Cuisines: Chinese, Buffet
Average price: Inexpensive
Address: 309 US Hwy 80 W
Savannah, GA 31408
Phone: (912) 964-2266

#297
Firehouse Subs
Cuisines: Sandwiches, Fast Food, Deli
Average price: Inexpensive
Address: 1935 East Victory Dr.
Savannah, GA 31404
Phone: (912) 354-3473

#298
Ming Garden Restaurant
Cuisines: Cafe
Average price: Inexpensive
Address: 2510 Montgomery St
Savannah, GA 31401
Phone: (912) 231-6688

#299
Carlito's Cuban Cabana
Cuisines: Cuban, Latin American
Average price: Inexpensive
Address: 41 Whitaker St
Savannah, GA 31401
Phone: (912) 232-0009

#300
El Gallo Mexican Restaurant
Cuisines: Mexican
Average price: Inexpensive
Address: 821 King George Blvd
Savannah, GA 31419
Phone: (912) 961-5696

#301
Carlucci's Old Style Pizzeria
Cuisines: Pizza
Average price: Modest
Address: 108 Shipyard Rd
Savannah, GA 31406
Phone: (912) 355-3333

#302
Maine-ly Dawgs Cafe
Cuisines: Cafe, Desserts
Average price: Modest
Address: 205 E 37th St
Savannah, GA 31401
Phone: (912) 417-2219

#303
Marco's Pizza
Cuisines: Pizza
Average price: Modest
Address: 2208 E Derenne
Savannah, GA 31406
Phone: (912) 335-1230

#304
Kobe
Cuisines: Japanese, Sushi Bar, Salad
Average price: Modest
Address: 1040 King George Blvd
Savannah, GA 31419
Phone: (912) 927-2008

#305
Jalapeno's Mexican Restaurant
Cuisines: Mexican
Average price: Modest
Address: 8840 Abercorn St
Savannah, GA 31406
Phone: (912) 920-0704

#306
**Zaxby's Chicken Fingers
& Buffalo Wings**
Cuisines: Fast Food, Chicken Wings, Salad
Average price: Modest
Address: 8040 White Bluff Rd
Savannah, GA 31406
Phone: (912) 927-6000

#307
Chick-fil-A
Cuisines: Fast Food
Average price: Inexpensive
Address: 2111 E Victory Dr
Savannah, GA 31404
Phone: (912) 352-7474

#308
Chef Charlotte's Confections
Cuisines: Bakery, Deli, Gluten-Free
Average price: Inexpensive
Address: 140 Johnny Mercer Blvd
Savannah, GA 31410
Phone: (912) 657-2927

#309
La Nopalera
Cuisines: Mexican
Average price: Inexpensive
Address: 108 Mall Blvd
Savannah, GA 31406
Phone: (912) 354-0300

#310
Siciliano's
Cuisines: Italian
Average price: Inexpensive
Address: 4700 E Hwy 80
Savannah, GA 31410
Phone: (912) 897-2715

#311
Friendship Coffee Company
Cuisines: Cafe
Average price: Inexpensive
Address: 205 Johnny Mercer Boulevard
Savannah, GA 31410
Phone: (912) 631-9544

#312
Rio Bravo Mexican Restaurant
Cuisines: Mexican
Average price: Modest
Address: 444 Johnny Mercer Blvd
Savannah, GA 31410
Phone: (912) 898-2300

#313
Castaways Sandfly
Cuisines: Sports Bar, Burgers,
Chicken Wings
Average price: Modest
Address: 7360 Skidaway Rd
Savannah, GA 31406
Phone: (912) 354-8288

#314
Domino's Pizza
Cuisines: Pizza, Chicken Wings, Sandwiches
Average price: Inexpensive
Address: 1900 E Victory Dr
Savannah, GA 31404
Phone: (912) 651-6001

#315
Taco Bell
Cuisines: Fast Food, Mexican, Tex-Mex
Average price: Inexpensive
Address: 2631 Skidaway Rd
Savannah, GA 31404
Phone: (912) 236-6682

#316
LongHorn Steakhouse
Cuisines: Steakhouse, American, Barbeque
Average price: Modest
Address: 7825 Abercorn Expy
Savannah, GA 31406
Phone: (912) 352-4784

#317
Rachael's 1190
Cuisines: American, Burgers, Pizza
Average price: Modest
Address: 1190 King George Blvd
Savannah, GA 31419
Phone: (912) 920-7772

#318
Buffalo Wild Wings
Cuisines: Chicken Wings,
Sports Bar, American
Average price: Modest
Address: 7700 Abercorn St
Savannah, GA 31405
Phone: (912) 355-6937

#319
Chili's
Cuisines: Bar, American, Tex-Mex
Average price: Modest
Address: 7805 Abercorn St
Savannah, GA 31406
Phone: (912) 352-3636

#320
Seasons of Japan
Cuisines: Japanese, Sushi Bar
Average price: Inexpensive
Address: 7400 Abercorn St
Savannah, GA 31406
Phone: (912) 353-9281

#321
Chick-fil-A
Cuisines: Fast Food
Average price: Inexpensive
Address: 303 Mall Blvd
Savannah, GA 31406
Phone: (912) 354-4355

#322
Atlanta Bread
Cuisines: Bakery, Sandwiches, Coffee & Tea
Average price: Inexpensive
Address: 5500 Abercorn Street
Savannah, GA 31405
Phone: (912) 691-1949

#323
The Village Bar and Grill
Cuisines: Bar, Burgers, Sandwiches
Average price: Modest
Address: 3 Skidaway Village Walk
Savannah, GA 31411
Phone: (912) 598-5106

#324
Romano's Macaroni Grill
Cuisines: Italian
Average price: Modest
Address: 7804 Abercorn
Savannah, GA 31406
Phone: (912) 692-1488

#325
Wing Zone
Cuisines: Chicken Wings
Average price: Inexpensive
Address: 1100 Eisenhower Dr
Savannah, GA 31406
Phone: (912) 354-8888

#326
China Taste
Cuisines: Chinese
Average price: Inexpensive
Address: 1040 King George Blvd
Savannah, GA 31419
Phone: (912) 920-2558

#327
Osaka
Cuisines: Cafe
Average price: Inexpensive
Address: 4749 Waters Ave
Savannah, GA 31404
Phone: (912) 353-8818

#328
Taste of India
Cuisines: Vegetarian, Indian
Average price: Modest
Address: 401 Mall Blvd
Savannah, GA 31406
Phone: (912) 356-1020

#329
Heiwa's
Cuisines: Japanese, Sushi Bar
Average price: Modest
Address: 7640 Abercorn St
Savannah, GA 31406
Phone: (912) 352-3838

#330
Larry's Giant Subs
Cuisines: Sandwiches
Average price: Inexpensive
Address: 4745 Waters Ave
Savannah, GA 31404
Phone: (912) 692-0807

#331
**Baraka's Homestyle Soul
& Seafood Restaurant**
Cuisines: Seafood, Soul Food
Average price: Inexpensive
Address: 1801 Waters Ave
Savannah, GA 31404
Phone: (912) 495-5447

#332
Molly McGuire's
Cuisines: Pub, Seafood
Average price: Modest
Address: 216 Johnny Mercer Blvd
Savannah, GA 31410
Phone: (912) 898-0852

#333
New China Garden Restaurant
Cuisines: Grocery, Asian Fusion
Average price: Inexpensive
Address: 12322 Largo Dr
Savannah, GA 31419
Phone: (912) 920-3028

#334
Sushi Time Towa
Cuisines: Japanese, Sushi Bar
Average price: Modest
Address: 54 W Montgomery Xrd
Savannah, GA 31406
Phone: (912) 920-3288

#335
Basil's Pizza & Deli
Cuisines: Pizza, Desserts, Sandwiches
Average price: Modest
Address: 216 Johnny Mercer Blvd
Savannah, GA 31410
Phone: (912) 897-6400

#336
Marco's Pizza
Cuisines: Pizza
Average price: Exclusive
Address: 50 Berwick Blvd
Savannah, GA 31419
Phone: (912) 234-6996

#337
Moe's Southwest Grill
Cuisines: Tex-Mex, Mexican
Average price: Inexpensive
Address: 150 West St Julian St
Savannah, GA 31401
Phone: (912) 335-2520

#338
Olive Garden Italian Restaurant
Cuisines: Italian, Salad, Wine Bar
Average price: Modest
Address: 11333 Abercorn St
Savannah, GA 31419
Phone: (912) 961-9009

#339
Cici's Pizza
Cuisines: Pizza
Average price: Inexpensive
Address: 7400 Abercorn St
Savannah, GA 31406
Phone: (912) 691-2777

#340
Ele Fine Fusion
Cuisines: Asian Fusion
Average price: Expensive
Address: 7815 US Hwy 80 E
Savannah, GA 31410
Phone: (912) 898-2221

#341
Ruan Thai Cuisine
Cuisines: Thai
Average price: Modest
Address: 17 W Broughton St
Savannah, GA 31401
Phone: (912) 231-6667

#342
Stoner's Pizza Joint
Cuisines: Pizza, Italian, Sandwiches
Average price: Expensive
Address: 1190 King George Blvd
Savannah, GA 31419
Phone: (912) 436-6117

#343
Sunnyside Up
Cuisines: Cafe
Average price: Inexpensive
Address: 800 E De Renne Ave
Savannah, GA 31405
Phone: (912) 354-2289

#344
Tortuga's Island Grille
Cuisines: Southern
Average price: Modest
Address: 2815 River Dr
Thunderbolt, GA 31404
Phone: (912) 201-3630

#345
Sam Snead's Tavern
Cuisines: Steakhouse, Sandwiches
Average price: Modest
Address: 7 Sylvester C Formey D
Savannah, GA 31408
Phone: (912) 963-0797

#346
Cilantro's
Cuisines: Bar, Mexican
Average price: Modest
Address: 461 Johnny Mercer Blvd
Savannah, GA 31410
Phone: (912) 232-7070

#347
Panera Bread
Cuisines: Sandwiches, Salad, Soup
Average price: Modest
Address: 1 W Broughton Street
Savannah, GA 31401
Phone: (912) 236-0275

#348
Firehouse Subs
Cuisines: Sandwiches, Fast Food, Deli
Average price: Inexpensive
Address: 8108 Abercorn St.
Savannah, GA 31406
Phone: (912) 920-4161

#349
Houlihan's
Cuisines: Bar, American
Average price: Modest
Address: 17029 Abercorn Street
Savannah, GA 31419
Phone: (912) 921-5712

#350
Eli's Restaurant
Cuisines: Cafe
Average price: Modest
Address: 15 Martin Luther King Blvd
Savannah, GA 31401
Phone: (912) 790-1000

#351
Northern Chick Express
Cuisines: Fast Food, Chicken Wings
Average price: Inexpensive
Address: 3125 Skidaway
Savannah, GA 31404
Phone: (912) 257-7163

#352
Sakura Place Japanese Restaurant
Cuisines: Japanese
Average price: Inexpensive
Address: 1190 King George Blvd
Savannah, GA 31419
Phone: (912) 961-0071

#353
Marco's Pizza
Cuisines: Pizza
Average price: Inexpensive
Address: 4521 Habersham St
Savannah, GA 31405
Phone: (912) 349-6960

#354
Green Tea 168 Restaurant
Cuisines: Chinese
Average price: Inexpensive
Address: 5730 Ogeechee Rd
Savannah, GA 31405
Phone: (912) 236-9488

#355
Krystal Burger
Cuisines: Burgers
Average price: Inexpensive
Address: 2804 Bee Rd
Savannah, GA 31404
Phone: (912) 352-4598

#356
Jennoely's Pizza
Cuisines: Pizza
Average price: Inexpensive
Address: Waters Ave
Savannah, GA
Phone: (912) 897-5309

#357
Panda Express
Cuisines: Chinese, Fast Food
Average price: Inexpensive
Address: 318 Mall Blvd
Savannah, GA 31406
Phone: (912) 692-8966

#358
BowTie Barbecue
Cuisines: Southern, American, Barbeque
Average price: Modest
Address: 6724 Waters Ave
Savannah, GA 31406
Phone: (912) 354-8828

#359
Jersey's Pizza
Cuisines: Pizza
Average price: Inexpensive
Address: 4827 Waters Ave
Savannah, GA 31404
Phone: (912) 354-2356

#360
Red Lobster
Cuisines: Seafood, American
Average price: Modest
Address: 11 W Montgomery Cross Roads
Savannah, GA 31406
Phone: (912) 927-1450

#361
Waffle House
Cuisines: American
Average price: Inexpensive
Address: 7301 Abercorn St
Savannah, GA 31406
Phone: (912) 354-4333

#362
Yummy House
Cuisines: Chinese
Average price: Inexpensive
Address: 111 Jazie Dr
Savannah, GA 31410
Phone: (912) 897-1900

#363
Zaxby's Chicken Fingers & Buffalo Wings
Cuisines: Fast Food, Chicken Wings, Salad
Average price: Inexpensive
Address: 1935 E Montgomery Cross Rd
Savannah, GA 31406
Phone: (912) 356-0406

#364
Moe's Southwest Grill
Cuisines: Tex-Mex, Mexican
Average price: Inexpensive
Address: 7801 Abercorn St
Savannah, GA 31406
Phone: (912) 303-6688

#365
Carey Hilliard's
Cuisines: American
Average price: Modest
Address: 11111 Abercorn St
Savannah, GA 31419
Phone: (912) 925-2131

#366
Happy China II
Cuisines: Chinese
Average price: Inexpensive
Address: 2022 Capital St
Savannah, GA 31404
Phone: (912) 238-8318

#367
York Street Deli
Cuisines: Deli, Breakfast & Brunch
Average price: Modest
Address: 114 Horizon Park Dr
Savannah, GA 31405
Phone: (912) 236-5195

#368
Mc Donalds
Cuisines: Burgers
Average price: Inexpensive
Address: 246 W Broughton St
Savannah, GA 31401
Phone: (912) 236-4494

#369
Wendy's
Cuisines: Fast Food, Burgers
Average price: Inexpensive
Address: 5321 Waters Ave
Savannah, GA 31404
Phone: (912) 354-3658

#370
Waffle House
Cuisines: American, Diner
Average price: Inexpensive
Address: 10002 Abercorn St
Savannah, GA 31406
Phone: (912) 927-2667

#371
Krystal Company
Cuisines: American
Average price: Inexpensive
Address: 5405 Abercorn St
Savannah, GA 31405
Phone: (912) 354-8893

#372
Larry's Giant Subs
Cuisines: Sandwiches, Greek
Average price: Inexpensive
Address: 7805 Abercorn St
Savannah, GA 31406
Phone: (912) 352-2441

#373
Chick-fil-A
Cuisines: Fast Food
Average price: Inexpensive
Address: 11152 Abercorn St
Savannah, GA 31419
Phone: (912) 921-0909

#374
Costanzo's Pizza
Cuisines: Pizza
Average price: Inexpensive
Address: 1100 Eisenhower Dr
Savannah, GA 31406
Phone: (912) 351-2400

#375
Larry's Giant Subs
Cuisines: American, Sandwiches
Average price: Inexpensive
Address: 2 Park of Commrce Blvd
Savannah, GA 31405
Phone: (912) 443-9440

#376
Papa Murphy's
Cuisines: Pizza
Average price: Modest
Address: 830 East Derenne Ave
Savannah, GA 31405
Phone: (912) 201-3021

#377
Piccadilly Cafeteria
Cuisines: American
Average price: Modest
Address: 7804 Abercorn St
Savannah, GA 31406
Phone: (912) 352-3521

#378
Costanzo's Pizzeria
Cuisines: Pizza
Average price: Modest
Address: 101 Little Neck Rd
Savannah, GA 31419
Phone: (912) 925-2006

#379
Baldinos Giant Jersey Subs
Cuisines: Cafe
Average price: Inexpensive
Address: 1800A E Victory Dr
Savannah, GA 31404
Phone: (912) 233-6506

#380
Season's of Japan
Cuisines: Japanese, Sushi Bar
Average price: Modest
Address: 50 Berwick Blvd
Savannah, GA 31419
Phone: (912) 234-2645

#381
La Salsa Grociers
Cuisines: Cafe
Average price: Inexpensive
Address: 147 Main St
Savannah, GA 31408
Phone: (912) 964-1575

#382
Jimmy John's
Cuisines: Sandwiches
Average price: Inexpensive
Address: 7 E Congress St
Savannah, GA 31401
Phone: (912) 234-8788

#383
Ruby Tuesday
Cuisines: Burgers, American
Average price: Modest
Address: 14045 Abercorn Street
Savannah, GA 31419
Phone: (912) 925-0193

#384
McDonald's
Cuisines: Burgers, Fast Food
Average price: Inexpensive
Address: 2701 Montgomery St
Savannah, GA 31405
Phone: (912) 233-5508

#385
Cookie Bar
Cuisines: Salad, Bar, Cafe
Average price: Modest
Address: 6700 Waters Ave
Savannah, GA 31406
Phone: (912) 291-2973

#386
Subway
Cuisines: Sandwiches, Fast Food
Average price: Inexpensive
Address: 1100 Eisenhower Dr
Savannah, GA 31406
Phone: (912) 303-9050

#387
Jimmy John's
Cuisines: Sandwiches
Average price: Inexpensive
Address: 11605 Abercorn St
Savannah, GA 31419
Phone: (912) 961-4098

#388
Wendy's
Cuisines: Fast Food, Burgers
Average price: Inexpensive
Address: 2020 E Victory Dr
Savannah, GA 31404
Phone: (912) 234-2819

#389
The Shellhouse Restaurant
Cuisines: Seafood
Average price: Modest
Address: 8 Gateway Blvd W
Savannah, GA 31419
Phone: (912) 927-3280

#390
HoneyBaked Ham of Savannah, GA
Cuisines: Meat Shop, Caterer, Sandwiches
Average price: Modest
Address: 8608-D Abercorn St
Savannah, GA 31406
Phone: (912) 920-7400

#391
China Star Restaurant
Cuisines: Chinese
Average price: Inexpensive
Address: 1163 Wheaton St
Savannah, GA 31404
Phone: (912) 232-4328

#392
Costanzo's Pizza
Cuisines: Pizza
Average price: Inexpensive
Address: 4827 Waters Ave
Savannah, GA 31404
Phone: (912) 354-2356

#393
Waffle House
Cuisines: American, Waffles
Average price: Modest
Address: 3711 Ogeechee Rd
Savannah, GA 31405
Phone: (912) 233-4480

#394
Loc Burger
Cuisines: Burgers, Sandwiches
Average price: Inexpensive
Address: 309 Main St
Garden City, GA 31408
Phone: (912) 235-0581

#395
Mardi Gras on Bay
Cuisines: Cajun/Creole
Average price: Modest
Address: 11 W Bay St
Savannah, GA 31401
Phone: (912) 234-0006

#396
El Potro Mexican Restaurant
Cuisines: Mexican
Average price: Modest
Address: 13051 Abercorn St
Savannah, GA 31419
Phone: (912) 927-9953

#397
Chef Wan Chinese Restaurant
Cuisines: Chinese
Average price: Inexpensive
Address: 342 Johnny Mercer Blvd
Savannah, GA 31410
Phone: (912) 897-0208

#398
The Krystal Co.
Cuisines: Burgers
Average price: Modest
Address: 14020 Abercorn St
Savannah, GA 31419
Phone: (912) 927-8890

#399
Domino's Pizza
Cuisines: Pizza, Chicken Wings, Sandwiches
Average price: Inexpensive
Address: 1101 E Montgomery Xrd
Savannah, GA 31406
Phone: (912) 921-0030

#400
Popeyes
Cuisines: Chicken Wings, Fast Food
Average price: Inexpensive
Address: 2060 E Victory Dr
Savannah, GA 31404
Phone: (912) 238-0420

#401
KFC
Cuisines: Fast Food, Chicken Wings
Average price: Inexpensive
Address: 19 Mersy Way
Savannah, GA 31405
Phone: (912) 239-1408

#402
Bone Fish Grill
Cuisines: Seafood
Average price: Modest
Address: 5500 Abercorn St
Savannah, GA 31405
Phone: (912) 691-2575

#403
The Jockey Club
Cuisines: American
Average price: Modest
Address: 5 E Public Sq
Washington, GA 30673
Phone: (706) 678-1672

#404
Checkers
Cuisines: American
Average price: Inexpensive
Address: 2510 Skidaway Rd
Savannah, GA 31404
Phone: (912) 236-8481

#405
Jennoely's Pizza
Cuisines: Pizza
Average price: Modest
Address: 140 Johnny Mercer Blvd
Savannah, GA 31410
Phone: (912) 898-3522

#406
Golden Corral Buffet & Grill
Cuisines: Buffet
Average price: Modest
Address: 7822 Abercorn St
Savannah, GA 31406
Phone: (912) 925-1274

#407
Cancun Mexican Restaurant
Cuisines: Mexican
Average price: Modest
Address: 216 Johnny Mercer Blvd
Savannah, GA 31410
Phone: (912) 898-0505

#408
Zaxby's Chicken Fingers
& Buffalo Wings
Cuisines: Fast Food, Chicken Wings, Salad
Average price: Inexpensive
Address: 5971 Ogeechee Rd
Savannah, GA 31419
Phone: (912) 961-5570

#409
Heiwa's Sushi Bar
& Teppan Yaki Grill
Cuisines: Sushi Bar, Japanese
Average price: Modest
Address: 7401 Skidaway Rd
Savannah, GA 31406
Phone: (912) 355-8819

#410
Checkers
Cuisines: Fast Food
Average price: Inexpensive
Address: 100 W De Renne Ave
Savannah, GA 31405
Phone: (912) 354-4939

#411
Hirano's Southside
Cuisines: Japanese
Average price: Modest
Address: 13015 Abercorn St
Savannah, GA 31419
Phone: (912) 961-0770

#412
China Buffet
Cuisines: Chinese
Average price: Inexpensive
Address: 1100 Eisenhower Dr
Savannah, GA 31406
Phone: (912) 355-9808

#413
Hibachi Grill & Supreme Buffet
Cuisines: Buffet, Chinese, Japanese
Average price: Inexpensive
Address: 220 Eisenhower Dr
Savannah, GA 31406
Phone: (912) 355-7878

#414
Bobby's Hometown Restaurant
Cuisines: Southern
Average price: Inexpensive
Address: 10 Engineering Dr
Savannah, GA 31407
Phone: (912) 966-7998

#415
El Fogon Katracho
Cuisines: Spanish
Average price: Inexpensive
Address: 1550 Dean Forest Rd
Garden City, GA 31408
Phone: (912) 964-1243

#416
Taco Bell
Cuisines: Mexican, Tex-Mex, Fast Food
Average price: Inexpensive
Address: 302 Mall Blvd
Savannah, GA 31406
Phone: (912) 355-5225

#417
Los Bravos
Cuisines: Mexican
Average price: Modest
Address: 1108 E Hwy 80
Pooler, GA 31322
Phone: (912) 748-4333

#418
Applebee's
Cuisines: American, Sports Bar, Burgers
Average price: Modest
Address: 11120 Abercorn St
Savannah, GA 31419
Phone: (912) 920-7966

#419
McDonald's
Cuisines: Fast Food, Burgers
Average price: Inexpensive
Address: 4306 Ogeechee Rd
Savannah, GA 31405
Phone: (912) 233-3266

#420
Baldinos Giant Jersey Subs
Cuisines: Sandwiches
Average price: Inexpensive
Address: 4620 Augusta Rd
Savannah, GA 31408
Phone: (912) 964-0133

#421
Applebee's
Cuisines: American, Sports Bar, Burgers
Average price: Modest
Address: 5460 Augusta Rd
Savannah, GA 31408
Phone: (912) 966-5030

#422
Smokey's BBQ
Cuisines: Barbeque
Average price: Modest
Address: 4118 Augusta Rd
Garden City, GA 31408
Phone: (912) 349-0864

#423
Yutaka Japanese Restaurant
Cuisines: Japanese
Average price: Inexpensive
Address: 5200 Augusta Rd
Savannah, GA 31408
Phone: (912) 964-2828

#424
Sonic Drive In Restaurant
Cuisines: Fast Food
Average price: Inexpensive
Address: 303 E Montgomery Cross Rd
Savannah, GA 31406
Phone: (912) 921-0303

#425
Burger King
Cuisines: Cafe
Average price: Inexpensive
Address: 4241 Augusta Rd
Savannah, GA 31408
Phone: (912) 964-5929

#426
Krystal
Cuisines: Fast Food
Average price: Inexpensive
Address: 4814 Augusta Rd
Savannah, GA 31408
Phone: (912) 964-6872

#427
Taco Bell
Cuisines: Fast Food, Mexican, Tex-Mex
Average price: Inexpensive
Address: 14005 Abercorn St
Savannah, GA 31419
Phone: (912) 925-0063

#428
Flacos Tacos
Cuisines: Mexican
Average price: Inexpensive
Address: 1117 S Rogers St
Pooler, GA 31322
Phone: (912) 988-7360

#429
Popeyes
Cuisines: Fast Food
Average price: Inexpensive
Address: 2514 Bull St
Savannah, GA 31401
Phone: (912) 234-8028

#430
Arby's
Cuisines: Fast Food, Sandwiches
Average price: Inexpensive
Address: 307 Mall Blvd
Savannah, GA 31406
Phone: (912) 354-8657

#431
Dickey's Barbecue Pit
Cuisines: Barbeque
Average price: Inexpensive
Address: 1109 US Hwy 80 E
Pooler, GA 31302
Phone: (912) 988-1286

#432
Tropical Chicken
Cuisines: Caribbean
Average price: Inexpensive
Address: 12313 Largo Dr
Savannah, GA 31419
Phone: (912) 961-5545

#433
Waffle House
Cuisines: American, Waffles
Average price: Modest
Address: 4310 Augusta Rd
Savannah, GA 31408
Phone: (912) 964-7657

#434
MoBay Island Cuisine
Cuisines: Caribbean, American
Average price: Modest
Address: 107 US Hwy 80 SE
Pooler, GA 31322
Phone: (912) 200-6834

#435
Papa John's Pizza
Cuisines: Pizza
Average price: Modest
Address: 2119 E Victory Dr
Savannah, GA 31404
Phone: (912) 352-8500

#436
Famous Asian Restaurant
Cuisines: Asian Fusion
Average price: Inexpensive
Address: 1450 Dean Forest Rd
Garden City, GA 31405
Phone: (912) 232-4250

#437
Five Guys
Cuisines: Burgers, Fast Food
Average price: Modest
Address: 4690 US Hwy 80 E
Savannah, GA 31410
Phone: (912) 898-0033

#438
Outback Steakhouse
Cuisines: Steakhouse
Average price: Modest
Address: 11196 Abercorn St
Savannah, GA 31419
Phone: (912) 920-0555

#439
Krystal
Cuisines: American, Fast Food
Average price: Inexpensive
Address: 10003 Abercorn St
Savannah, GA 31406
Phone: (912) 925-0906

#440
Dewar's Clubhouse Bar & Grille
Cuisines: American, Bar
Average price: Modest
Address: 400 Airways Ave
Savannah, GA 31408
Phone: (912) 964-7227

#441
Pizza Hut
Cuisines: Pizza
Average price: Modest
Address: 2405 Skidaway Rd
Savannah, GA 31404
Phone: (912) 236-6070

#442
Babe's at the Market
Cuisines: American
Average price: Inexpensive
Address: 701 US Hwy 80 W
Garden City, GA 31408
Phone: (912) 964-1492

#443
KFC
Cuisines: Chicken Wings, Fast Food
Average price: Inexpensive
Address: 11502 Abercorn Extension
Savannah, GA 31419
Phone: (912) 927-0506

#444
Sonic Drive-In
Cuisines: Fast Food
Average price: Inexpensive
Address: 4301 Ogeechee Rd
Savannah, GA 31405
Phone: (912) 233-6330

#445
Love's Seafood & Steaks
Cuisines: Seafood, American, Steakhouse
Average price: Modest
Address: 6817 Chief Of Love Rd
Savannah, GA 31419
Phone: (912) 925-3616

#446
Sunrise Restaurant
Cuisines: Buffet
Average price: Inexpensive
Address: 346 Johnny Mercer Blvd
Savannah, GA 31410
Phone: (912) 897-2899

#447
Sunny Side Up
Cuisines: Breakfast & Brunch, American
Average price: Modest
Address: 4800 Augusta Rd
Garden City, GA 31408
Phone: (912) 964-9898

#448
McDonald's
Cuisines: Fast Food, Burgers
Average price: Inexpensive
Address: 2025 Skidaway Rd
Savannah, GA 31404
Phone: (912) 234-1649

#449
China House
Cuisines: Chinese
Average price: Modest
Address: 205 S Coastal Hwy
Savannah, GA 31407
Phone: (912) 964-7733

#450
Papa John's Pizza
Cuisines: Pizza
Average price: Modest
Address: 11613 Abercorn St
Savannah, GA 31419
Phone: (912) 920-2500

#451
Jersey Mike's Subs
Cuisines: Fast Food, Deli, Sandwiches
Average price: Inexpensive
Address: 7400 Abercorn St.
Savannah, GA 31406
Phone: (912) 355-3077

#452
Splendid Shabu
Cuisines: Hot Pot, Asian Fusion, Chinese
Average price: Modest
Address: 9 Mill Creek Cir
Pooler, GA 31322
Phone: (912) 348-2242

#453
Perkins Restaurant & Bakery
Cuisines: Bakery, American
Average price: Modest
Address: 3A Gateway Blvd S
Savannah, GA 31419
Phone: (912) 961-0424

#454
Godfathers Pizza
Cuisines: Pizza
Average price: Inexpensive
Address: 8303 White Bluff Rd
Savannah, GA 31406
Phone: (912) 925-9303

#455
Pie Society
Cuisines: British, Bakery
Average price: Inexpensive
Address: 115 Canal St
Pooler, GA 31322
Phone: (912) 856-4785

#456
McDonald's
Cuisines: Burgers, Fast Food
Average price: Inexpensive
Address: 600 E De Renne Ave
Savannah, GA 31405
Phone: (912) 352-3481

#457
Little Caesars Pizza
Cuisines: Pizza
Average price: Inexpensive
Address: 8501 Waters Ave
Savannah, GA 31406
Phone: (912) 349-6283

#458
McDonald's
Cuisines: Fast Food, Burgers
Average price: Inexpensive
Address: 13100 Abercorn St
Savannah, GA 31419
Phone: (912) 927-0876

#459
Cracker Barrel Old Country Store
Cuisines: American
Average price: Inexpensive
Address: 17017 Abercorn St
Savannah, GA 31419
Phone: (912) 927-6559

#460
McDonald's
Cuisines: Fast Food, Burgers
Average price: Inexpensive
Address: 6740 Waters Ave
Savannah, GA 31406
Phone: (912) 356-1219

#461
Sonic Drive-In
Cuisines: Fast Food
Average price: Inexpensive
Address: 5440 Augusta Rd
Savannah, GA 31408
Phone: (912) 964-8002

#462
Hercule's Bar & Grill
Cuisines: Bar, Pizza, Burgers
Average price: Modest
Address: 2500 Dean Forest Rd
Garden, GA 31408
Phone: (912) 966-5790

#463
McDonald's
Cuisines: Fast Food, Burgers
Average price: Inexpensive
Address: 7979 White Bluff Rd
Savannah, GA 31406
Phone: (912) 961-1878

#464
Subway
Cuisines: Sandwiches, Fast Food
Average price: Inexpensive
Address: 131 E Broughton St
Savannah, GA 31401
Phone: (912) 239-0093

#465
Smokin Pig
Cuisines: Barbeque
Average price: Inexpensive
Address: 1215 Hwy 80 E
Pooler, GA 31322
Phone: (912) 330-0192

#466
Happy Wok
Cuisines: Chinese
Average price: Inexpensive
Address: 7306 Ga Hwy 21
Savannah, GA 31407
Phone: (912) 966-3030

#467
Dairy Queen
Cuisines: Fast Food, Ice Cream
Average price: Inexpensive
Address: 5004 Augusta Rd
Savannah, GA 31408
Phone: (912) 966-0868

#468
Hooters
Cuisines: Sports Bar, Chicken Wings
Average price: Modest
Address: 4 Gateway Boulevard, West
Savannah, GA 31409
Phone: (912) 925-2536

#469
Sonic
Cuisines: Fast Food
Average price: Inexpensive
Address: 1020 King George Blvd
Savannah, GA 31419
Phone: (912) 927-6777

#470
Happy China 3
Cuisines: Chinese
Average price: Inexpensive
Address: 10 Quacco Rd
Savannah, GA 31419
Phone: (912) 961-1054

#471
Sonic Drive In Restaurant
Cuisines: Fast Food
Average price: Modest
Address: 4691 US Hwy 80 E
Savannah, GA 31410
Phone: (912) 897-1122

#472
Jalapenos Mexican Grill
Cuisines: Mexican
Average price: Inexpensive
Address: 107 Charlotte Dr
Savannah, GA 31410
Phone: (912) 897-8245

#473
Sweet Spice Restaurant & Bar
Cuisines: Caribbean
Average price: Modest
Address: 1024 US Hwy 80w
Pooler, GA 31322
Phone: (912) 348-3176

#474
Chuck E Cheese's
Cuisines: Pizza
Average price: Modest
Address: 6700 Abercorn St
Savannah, GA 31405
Phone: (912) 355-0410

#475
Pizza Hut
Cuisines: Pizza, Italian, Chicken Wings
Average price: Inexpensive
Address: 4717 US Highway 80 E
Savannah, GA 31410
Phone: (912) 898-1213

#476
Phillips Famous Seafood
Cuisines: Seafood
Average price: Modest
Address: 400 Airways Ave
Savannah, GA 31408
Phone: (757) 858-9601

#477
Pizza Hut
Cuisines: Pizza, Italian, Chicken Wings
Average price: Modest
Address: 40 East DeRenne Ave, Ste. 40
Savannah, GA 31405
Phone: (912) 353-8300

#478
Pizza Hut
Cuisines: Pizza, Italian, Chicken Wings
Average price: Modest
Address: 5730 Ogeechee Road
Savannah, GA 31405
Phone: (912) 233-2886

#479
Southbridge Golf Club
Cuisines: Cafe
Average price: Modest
Address: 415 Southbridge Blvd
Savannah, GA 31405
Phone: (912) 651-5455

#480
Wendy's
Cuisines: Fast Food, Burgers
Average price: Inexpensive
Address: 112 Mall Blvd
Savannah, GA 31406
Phone: (912) 352-2801

#481
Naan Appetit
Cuisines: Indian
Average price: Modest
Address: 1024 US 80 W
Pooler, GA 31322
Phone: (912) 348-2446

#482
Ruby Tuesday
Cuisines: American, Burgers
Average price: Modest
Address: 580 Al Henderson Blvd
Savannah, GA 31419
Phone: (912) 920-0128

#483
Mandarin Express
Cuisines: Indian
Average price: Inexpensive
Address: 7804 Abercorn St
Savannah, GA 31406
Phone: (912) 356-1621

#484
Applebee's
Cuisines: American, Sports Bar, Burgers
Average price: Modest
Address: 587 Al Henderson Blvd
Savannah, GA 31419
Phone: (912) 920-9199

#485
Waffle House
Cuisines: Diner, American
Average price: Modest
Address: 8 Stephen S Green Dr
Savannah, GA 31408
Phone: (912) 966-5424

#486
Two Brothers Pizza
Cuisines: Pizza, Sandwiches
Average price: Inexpensive
Address: 990 Pine Barren Rd
Pooler, GA 31322
Phone: (912) 450-8844